Birds

A huge bird swoops down.

In the blink of an eye it snatches a fish from the waters below, then flies…

Soaring with the Wind

THE BALD EAGLE

MORROW JUNIOR BOOKS
NEW YORK

GAIL GIBBONS

Watercolors, colored pencil, and black pen were used for the full-color illustrations. The text type is 14-point ITC Bookman.

Published by Morrow Junior Books
a division of William Morrow and Company, Inc.
1350 Avenue of the Americas, New York, NY 10019

Manufactured in China.

9 10

Library of Congress Cataloging-in-Publication Data

Gibbons, Gail.
Soaring with the wind: the bald eagle/Gail Gibbons.
p. cm.
Summary: Describes the characteristics, behavior, and life cycle of the bald eagle.
ISBN 0-688-13730-X (trade)—ISBN 0-688-13731-8 (library)
1. Bald eagle—Juvenile literature.   [1. Bald eagle.   2. Eagles.]   I. Title.
QL696.F32G5 1998   598.9'43—dc21   97-20497   CIP AC

To Rebecca and Eric, my grown-up children

The author wishes to thank Peter Nye, research scientist with the New York State Division of Fish and Wildlife, Delma, New York, for his expert help. Thanks also to Mike Owen of the Fakahatchee Strand State Preserve, Copeland, Florida.

CLAWS, also called TALONS

The bald eagle is a *raptor*. Raptors are birds of prey, which means they eat meat. The name *raptor* comes from the Latin word *rapere*, meaning "to grasp or seize by force." Bald eagles are excellent hunters, gripping their prey with claws, also called *talons*, that are razor sharp and four inches long.

A bald eagle isn't bald. Its name comes from *balde,* an Old English word meaning "white." With its gleaming white head and tail feathers, the bald eagle cannot be mistaken for any other bird. It belongs to the group of eagles called *fish and sea eagles* that lives near water and eats mostly fish and water birds.

An adult bald eagle is about three feet tall from head to tail and weighs about eleven pounds. Often the female is bigger than the male. They both have the same basic characteristics.

WING

CROWN

EYE

NECK

BEAK

THROAT

BREAST

BELLY

BACK

TAIL FEATHERS

FEET

TOE

LEG

A thin clear eyelid, the NICTITATING (NICK-TIH-TATE-ING) membrane, protects and cleans the eye.

The bald eagle is one of the largest hunting birds in North America. Its body is perfectly designed for flight and for catching prey. The entire skeleton of a bald eagle weighs only about half a pound. Each bone is hollow and filled with air.

BONE

BRACES, also called STRUTS, inside the bone give it strength.

FEATHER

There are about 7,000 feathers on a bald eagle's body. Together, they weigh a little less than one and one-half pounds. They overlap one another to create a lot of air space in between. This helps to *insulate*, or protect, the bird's body from heat and cold.

COVERT FEATHERS

HOOKED BARBULE

BOWED BARBULE

The strong PRIMARY FEATHERS can spread out like fingers on a hand to cause friction that slows the eagle down. This is called drag.

The SECONDARY FEATHERS can move down to increase drag or up to reduce it.

The COVERT FEATHERS shape the wing so that air moves faster over the top than under the bottom. The difference in air pressure gives the eagle better lift.

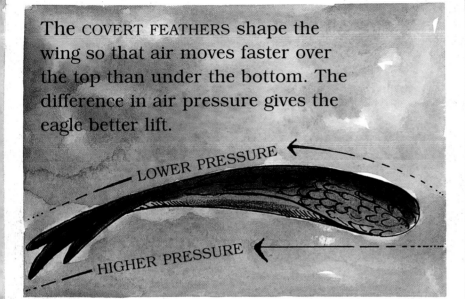

LOWER PRESSURE

HIGHER PRESSURE

An airplane's wing is shaped like a bird's wing.

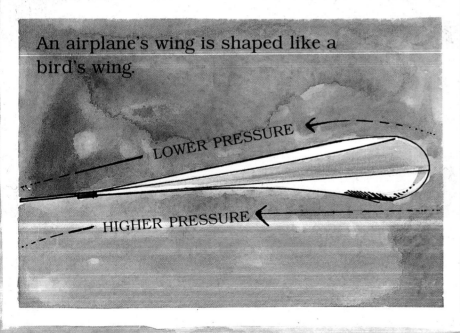

LOWER PRESSURE

HIGHER PRESSURE

The TAIL FEATHERS are used for stopping and steering.

The feathers are strong because they are made of *keratin*, just like your fingernails. Each feather is held together by a pattern of *barbules*. More than 350,000 tiny *hooked barbules* are attached to *bowed barbules* to give each feather its particular shape.

Like all birds, eagles are streamlined for flight. Their wingspread can be as wide as seven and a half feet. The wings are flatter on the bottom than on top, just like an airplane's wings. The bald eagle uses its wing feathers to lift off and change direction, and it can dive down through the air at 100 miles an hour!

When the bald eagle wants to soar far up into the sky, it often hitches a ride on rising hot-air currents called *thermals*. Once it gets into the thermal, the eagle spreads its long and narrow wings and floats like a hang glider. Sometimes a really big thermal can carry an eagle three miles above the earth!

When the sun warms the ground, the air above it rises. These rising warm-air currents are called THERMALS.

RESOLVING POWER is the ability to focus on things far away. A bald eagle has eight times more resolving power than a person.

Eagles only kill when they are hungry. Their golden eyes have amazing vision that can see objects up to two miles away. They can hear faraway sounds, too, like the splash of a fish. When an eagle finds its prey, it can spread its wings and float down so quietly that its victim can't hear it coming.

SPICULES, tiny spikes on the toes, help hold slippery prey.

A bald eagle can eat four to five fish a day. Besides water birds, it also eats rabbits and the carcasses of dead animals it finds. The bird is so strong, it can lift half its own body weight. Its sharp talons dig into and kill what it catches. Then it shreds and tears its prey apart with its sharp hook-shaped beak so its meal is easy to eat. Each eagle has its own hunting ground and may attack another eagle coming into its territory.

Bald eagles are found only in North America. Some eagles live and hunt in the same area all year-round, but most follow their prey when the seasons change. When winter sets in and snow and ice cover the land and waters, northern eagles fly south until they find open water and prey. In the spring they return to their breeding grounds in the north. This traveling back and forth is called *migration.* Some eagles migrate thousands of miles.

Where Bald Eagles Are Found

WINTER

SUMMER

YEAR-ROUND

CANADA

PACIFIC OCEAN

UNITED STATES

ATLANTIC OCEAN

MEXICO

Spring is mating season. Male and female eagles attract each other with a high-pitched call. They usually mate for life. They take a new mate only when their first mate dies. Once they've mated, eagles return to the same nesting territory year after year.

Before mating, there is a fascinating form of behavior called the courtship ritual. Some of it takes place in the air. A male and female chase each other, dive, and make loops. Sometimes high in the sky they lock their talons together and cartwheel downward. Just before touching ground they let go and fly upward again. During the spring some eagles spend more time and energy courting than hunting.

After courtship and mating, nest building begins. Bald eagles build the largest nests of any bird. Most are about six feet deep and six feet in diameter. A new nesting pair builds its nest in a high out-of-reach place, almost always in a tree. They weave twigs and large sticks together and line the nest with soft mosses, feathers, leaves, and grasses. Pairs that have been mates before add to and clean up their old nests. They build a new nest only if their old one has fallen down.

The nest is called an AERIE (AIR-EE).

INCUBATION
(IN-KEW-BAY-SHUN)

Female bald eagles lay one to three eggs. The male and female take turns sitting on the eggs to keep them warm. This is called *incubation*. While one sits on the eggs, its mate hunts for food and fiercely guards the nesting territory from intruders.

After about 35 days a peep comes from inside an egg. A chick is ready to hatch. It uses its *egg tooth* to peck its way out of the shell. This tiring struggle can take from a few hours to two days. Finally, the chick appears. The chick, called an *eaglet*, weighs about three ounces. It is helpless, wet, and tiny. One by one the other eggs hatch.

EGG TOOTH

EAGLET

BROODING means "caring for the young."

Brooding time has begun. The parents care for and feed the eaglets. One parent keeps them warm while the other hunts. The parents use their beaks to tear apart meat into pieces small enough for the eaglets to eat. These eaglets are two days old and covered in dry, fluffy down.

After about one month the eaglets have lost their first coat of down. Their new coat is thick and woolly. The eaglets are about ten times bigger than when they were born. When they are around two months old, their feathers have grown in. They practice flying by hopping up and down and hovering in the air. Their parents continue to feed and care for them.

FLEDGLING

Now they are four months old and fully grown. They fly out of the nest, gliding to nearby branches. Flying for the first time is called *fledging*. For the next two months the eaglets, now called *fledglings*, will stay with their parents and master their hunting skills.

In the fall the young eagles, now called *immatures*, fly south to join other migrating bald eagles. It will take about five years for them to develop the brilliant white head and tail feathers, as well as the bright golden eyes, of their parents. Then they will be ready to mate and raise their own young.

IMMATURE

Because of the fierce strength and beauty of the bald eagle, it has been a symbol in North America for centuries. Native Americans revere these birds, viewing them as sacred. Some have said that only a relative of the sun could soar so high into the clouds. In traditional beliefs, it is a bald eagle that pushes the sun across the sky, and it is the sun's great heat that turns the eagle's head and tail feathers white.

To many Native Americans, the bald eagle has special powers. They believe they will share in those powers by possessing the feathers or a part of this majestic bird. Great leaders have often worn eagle feathers in their headdresses, each feather standing for a brave deed, and eagle dances are performed at ceremonies. Another traditional belief is that prayers are carried up on eagles' wings to gods and spirits. Some tribes carve the image of the bald eagle at the top of totem poles, the place of highest respect.

In 1782 the bald eagle was chosen by the Continental Congress as the emblem of the United States of America. It represents strength, dignity, and freedom. Its image is found on coins, flags, monuments, and many other objects.

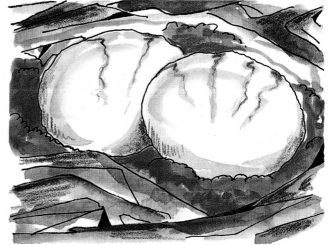

Once there were thousands of bald eagles in North America. Then people began hunting them for sport. Farmers shot them because they falsely believed bald eagles killed small farm animals and too many fish. Also, people moved into wilderness areas, cutting down trees and destroying the eagles' territory.

Then farmers sprayed their fields with a poison, called DDT, to protect their crops from pests. Rainwater carried the DDT into waterways, poisoning fish and other sources of the bald eagles' food. When eagles fed on prey that was contaminated with DDT, some died. Others laid eggs that never hatched, because DDT had made the eggshells so thin and soft.

In 1969 only a few hundred pairs of these birds were left in the lower 48 states. So the United States added the bald eagle to the nation's endangered species list. *Endangered* means "in danger of becoming *extinct.*" The government created laws to protect bald eagles, and it set aside land, called *sanctuaries,* where it is safe for bald eagles to live. Now it is illegal to kill or even to disturb a bald eagle.

In 1972 the use of DDT in the United States was banned, and in 1976 a number of state and private wildlife organizations began programs to restore eagles to the land. Eaglets are raised by humans in a safe natural environment that will eventually be their home— a process called *hacking.*

HACK TOWER

EXTINCT means "to no longer exist."

SANCTUARY

The number of bald eagles has increased ten times as a result of these efforts. In some areas they are no longer endangered. Instead, they are listed as *threatened,* which means they still need to be protected. If human beings can maintain safe and adequate places for them to live—which is the most important thing humans can do—bald eagles will go on being warriors of the sky, soaring with the wind.

Warriors of the Sky

- There are 59 kinds of eagles in the world. They are found on every continent except Antarctica. There are 11 kinds of fish and sea eagles.

- Falconers—people who train hawks for hunting—keep the birds in a state of partial liberty, called *at hack*, as they are being trained. The efforts of today's restoration programs are often known as *hacking*.

- The largest bald eagle nest ever seen weighed about 2,000 pounds, as much as a car.

- Some scientists and other people keep track of bald eagles by putting bands on the birds' legs. They want to make sure the eagle population continues to rise. These bands have different numbers on them to identify the different birds.

- The term *eagle eyed* means "to have good vision and notice things quickly."

- Often bald eagles catch weak and sick animals. That keeps the small-animal population healthy and our natural world in balance.

- In the United States, the first image of a bald eagle appeared on a document signed by George Washington after the Revolutionary War.

- In the wild a bald eagle can live to be about 40 years old. The adult eagle has no enemy except for people.

WARNING! Never approach the nest of a bald eagle. This may cause the birds to flee, leaving their eggs to grow cold. Watch them from far away with binoculars. They don't like to be disturbed.